FRANK
Lloyd Wright

THIS IS A CARLTON BOOK

Text and design copyright © 1999 Carlton Books Limited

This edition published by Carlton Books Limited 1999
20 St Anne's Court
Wardour Street
London
W1V 3AW

A CIP catalogue for this book is available from the British Library

ISBN 1 85868 754 3

EXECUTIVE EDITOR: Sarah Larter
MANAGING ART EDITOR: Zoë Mercer
DESIGN: Simon Mercer
PICTURE RESEARCH: Lorna Ainger
PRODUCTION: Garry Lewis

Printed and bound in Dubai

FRANK
Lloyd Wright

NAOMI STUNGO

CARLTON

Never has an architect

combined genius and infamy with such staggering aplomb as the American Frank Lloyd Wright. The model for numerous books, plays and films, including Ayn Rand's study of megalomania, *The Fountainhead*, Wright designed more than 1,000 buildings during his prolific 92-year lifetime, scandalized polite society continually with his outrageous private life, and declared himself not only the single-handed founder of modern architecture, but also the greatest architect – ever.

How you decide who is the world's greatest architect is far from clear. How do you rate Michaelangelo against the very different talent of Gaudì? What is gained by comparing Brunelleschi with Alvar Aalto? Certainly, a number of Wright's buildings rank among the world's most famous – the Guggenheim Museum in New York and the waterside summer house in Pennsylvania known as Fallingwater are internationally acclaimed. And yet, almost all of his architecture has huge technical faults: many of his buildings have leaked since the day they were completed; and, even as this is written, Fallingwater is being shored up, before it does, literally, fall into the water.

So, was Wright the inventor of modern architecture? Well, maybe. In his pioneering use of open-plan living spaces, his concern for the "honest" expression of materials, his interest in technology and his respect for nature, Wright anticipated almost all of the key themes that have dominated architecture in the twentieth century.

Born in Wisconsin in 1867, Frank Lincoln Wright – as he was christened – was the eldest child and only son of William Wright, a local minister and music teacher, and his wife Anna Lloyd Jones Wright. His strong-willed mother was a passionate and ambitious woman who channelled the frustrations of her unhappy marriage into pushing her young son. She had a formative influence over Wright: not only did he take her name as a teenager when his parents divorced, but in his autobiography, Wright credited her with determining the very direction of

FRANK LLO

his life, claiming that his mother had told him of a premonition she had while pregnant with him – her son was to become a great architect.

Whether or not this is true – and it smacks rather of the myth that Wright later built up around his life – Anna Wright certainly encouraged her son's early interest in architecture, decorating his nursery with prints of English cathedrals and teaching him to play with "Froebel" blocks. A teacher herself, she was fascinated with these new toys – coloured strips of paper, two dimensional geometric grids, wood spheres, blocks and pyramids – which were designed by the German educational philosopher Friedrich Froebel, the inventor of the kinder-garten. The toys, used in conjunction with a series of elaborate exercises, were intended to develop children's sensory experience of the world and seem to have had a profound influence on Wright. "I give you my word," Wright used to say, describing their effect on his thinking, "all those things are in my hands today – the feeling of those maple forms". Looking at Wright's architecture you see the Froebel shapes – the cube, the sphere, the pyramid and myriad combinations of all of them – recurring time and again. "There," he explained, "is the modular system that has been back [sic] of every design I ever made."

The Froebel system was more, however, than a mere set of spatial and analytical exercises; Froebel intended the toys to have symbolic and spiritual meaning. As William Cronon has explained, Froebel believed that certain key geometric forms symbolized human ideas, moods and sentiments – the circle, infinity; the triangle, structural unity; the spire, aspiration; the spiral, organic progress; the square, integrity. It sounds strange today, but the idea that a set of toys could teach children about the underlying principles of the cosmos was far from outlandish in the mid-nineteenth century. For Anna Wright, and later her son, the idea had huge appeal, tying in, as it did, with their Unitarian beliefs.

To understand Frank Lloyd Wright, you have to understand something of Unitarianism, the religion in which his family was steeped through and through. Wright's father was a Unitarian preacher, his mother descended from a long line of Welsh Unitarians who had settled in

YD WRIGHT

Wisconsin in the 1840s. Extreme liberal Protestants, they rejected almost every convention of the established church, stressing instead reason and conscience as the foundations of religion. Individuals, they believed, should seek out God for themselves in the world around them. The function of science and art was to help in this quest – hence children's toys should be vehicles for understanding the underlying principles of the universe and the nature of God.

Another important vehicle for Wright was the natural world itself. Nature is key theme in Wright's thinking and we see it recalled again and again in his designs – in decorative motifs such as stained glass, furnishings and fittings, as well as in his more general concern to site his buildings in harmony with their natural surroundings.

" I THINK Nature SHOULD BE SPELLED WITH A CAPITAL 'N', NOT BECAUSE NATURE IS GOD BUT BECAUSE ALL THAT WE CAN LEARN OF GOD WE WILL LEARN FROM THE BODY OF GOD, WHICH WE CALL NATURE. "

Wright's formal architectural training began at 18 when he enrolled in the engineering school at the University of Wisconsin in Madison. Ambitious and impatient in equal measure, he soon tired of small town life. For a young man passionate about architecture, the only place to be was clearly Chicago, the melting pot of technology and design. When Wright arrived in 1887 the city was in the throes of a building bonanza; the great fire of 1871 had destroyed huge swathes of the city which were now being rebuilt on a heroic scale thanks to the invention of the lift a few years earlier by Elisha Graves Otis.

Wright quickly sought out the most innovative architectural practice, Adler and Sullivan, where, despite his lack of experience, he was taken on as an assistant to Louis Sullivan. Here began one of the most formative experiences of Wright's long life. For, although they were later to fall out, Wright always recognized Sullivan as an exemplary teacher, referring to him as his *Lieber Meister* or "dear master". Certainly, it was an exciting office to work in; when Wright joined the practice Adler and Sullivan were engaged on the Auditorium Building, one of the most famous tall buildings of its time. Wright progressed quickly and was soon put in charge of the practice's residential work, so beginning his life-long passion for house design.

Wright honed his early style in a succession of remarkable houses built in the smart Chicago suburb of Oak Park. Like his *Lieber Meister*, Wright sought to create a new and authentic American architecture. Rejecting the fashionable Classical beaux-arts style of the time he set about developing an architecture in keeping with the vast expanses of the Midwest.

The first hints of this Prairie style, as it became known, appear in the Oak Park house (1889–1909) Wright designed for himself and his first wife, Catherine Lee Tobin. The couple married in 1889 and, borrowing money from Sullivan, Wright began the house that was to be home to the couple and their six children for the next ten years. With its low, ground-hugging proportions, horizontal emphasis and free-flowing interior spaces, the house was a radical departure from the mock-Tudor of most American suburbs.

Wright's solo career was abruptly launched in 1893, when Sullivan fired him for moonlighting. Hurriedly adding a drafting studio to the house, Wright quickly picked up commissions from wealthy Chicagans fleeing the windy city for the tranquil greenery of Oak Park. He was still only 26 when he designed the Winslow House (1893–1894), his first solo commission and the first true Prairie House.

"I LOVED THE **prairie** BY INSTINCT, AS A GREAT SIMPLICITY – THE TREES, THE FLOWERS, THE SKY ITSELF, THRILLING **CONTRAST**. I SAW THAT A LITTLE OF HEIGHT IN THE PRAIRIE WAS ENOUGH TO LOOK LIKE MUCH MORE – EVERY **detail** AS TO HEIGHT BECOMING IMMENSELY SIGNIFICANT, BREADTHS ALL FALLING SHORT ... I HAD AN IDEA THAT THE **HORIZONTAL PLANES** IN BUILDINGS BELONG TO THE GROUND. I BEGAN PUTTING THIS **idea** TO WORK."

When Daniel Burnham, the patriarch of Chicago architecture at the time, saw the Winslow House he offered to send Wright on a study trip to the Ecole des Beaux-Arts in Paris and on a grand tour of Italy. Burnham felt the house, while skilful, made no sense. Others agreed, even those with confidence in Wright. Indeed Wright's next client, Nathan G. Moore, came to him demanding a house as different from the Winslow house as possible, because he " [didn't] want to go down the backstreets to [his] morning train to avoid being laughed at."

Starkly unadorned, the Winslow House was revolutionary. Its low, hovering form rises directly from a raised plinth, so that the house seems to grow out of the ground. Instead of being plastered over, the cast concrete and brick is left bare, capped by a terracotta frieze, a gently oversailing roof and massive central chimney.

And yet the impetus for this new aesthetic was surely not all American. In 1893 Wright had visited the *Ho-o-den* exhibit at the World's Colombian Exposition, a reconstructed Japanese temple. Wright's reaction is not known, but the parallels between the flowing interior spaces, screen-like walls, overhanging eves and long, low roofs of Japanese architecture and Wright's emerging Prairie style are too striking to ignore. In later lifer life, Wright was certainly an avid Japanophile, living and working in Japan and amassing a valuable collection of Japanese art, so it seems legitimate to speculate that an interest in things Japanese was partly responsible for the increasingly unorthodox style of his work.

In the Unity Temple (1905–1908), the Unitarian chapel he designed for Oak Park, Wright experimented still further. The building is shockingly blank-looking from the outside, however, the interior is alive with light and movement. Pushing what he called the " destruction of the box" – the replacement of the boxy layout of most nineteenth-century buildings with a more free-flowing arrangement of space – Wright supported the weight of the building's immense glazed roof on four

" WE IN THE MIDDLE WEST ARE LIVING ON THE PRAIRIE. THE PRAIRIE HAS A **beauty** OF ITS OWN AND WE SHOULD RECOGNIZE AND ACCENTUATE THIS NATURAL BEAUTY, ITS **quiet** LEVEL. HENCE, GENTLY SLOPING ROOFS, LOW PROPORTIONS, QUIET **skylines**, SUPPRESSED HEAVY-SET CHIMNEYS AND SHELTERING OVERHANGS, LOW TERRACES. "

huge columns. As the walls were non load-bearing, they could be used as screens, pierced with high-level windows that bring light flooding into the building, while the interior spaces could be infinitely more fluid.

The Robie House (1908–1910) is the apotheosis of Wright's new, radical style. Hailed as the "house of the century" by *House and Home* magazine when threatened with demolition in 1958, it dissolves all interior space so that rooms become a string of pavilions linked by promenades and galleries. Massive and low, it became known, not surprisingly, as the "battleship". The deck-like lower floors house the playroom, billiard room and utility areas (at ground floor level) and the main living spaces (on the first floor), which flow seamlessly from one to the other. The bedrooms are above on the smaller third floor (the "poop deck" as it were) which, together with the heavy-set chimney, visually anchors the whole strange assembly. As with so many of his buildings, Wright also designed the furniture, using it to further his aims for the whole house. Extending the theme of openness to the dining room table, for example, he created a table with posts at the corners housing recessed vases and topped by lights so that guests and family would be able to see, uninterrupted, across the dinner table.

Only 33 years old when he commissioned Wright to design him a house, Frederick C. Robie was a talented young engineer and head of a company making bicycles. His house, he demanded, should run as smoothly as a machine. Looking at Wright's buildings today, it is difficult to imagine them as the pinnacle of technological achievement but, in their day, that is exactly what they were. For all his interest in nature, Wright was also a technocrat. The Robie House was the latest in fireproof houses, the Unity Temple used unpainted concrete as a cladding material for the first time, while the Larkin building pushed developments even further.

The Larkin Company Administration Building in Buffalo, New York (1903–1905), was demolished in 1950; if it were still standing today it would be an astonishing sight. And what must have been thought of it in 1905 one can only wonder. The Larkin Building was a revolutionary machine for working in. Wright's client, a soap-making and mail order tycoon, wanted a clean, delightful working environment that would foster good working relations between employer and employees. Wright rose to the task with a vengeance. Inside its cliff-like blank walls, the whole layout of the building was unique. Its dominant feature was a central atrium that, lit from above, was wrapped around by four floors of open galleries so that everyone could see everyone – employer and employee alike. Sited at its corners, leaving cross-views unimpaired, were four shafts that brought in high-level fresh air, heated it, and pumped it around the building. The building marked a series of "firsts": the steel desk furniture, the wall-hung toilets and the air conditioning were all utterly innovative.

Wright was now famous: immensely prolific, his buildings were attracting widespread interest, he had clients aplenty, he was earning well. But he was bored and, in 1909, he threw it all in, abandoning his wife and six children for Mamah Cheney, the freethinking feminist wife of a client and neighbour. Chicago society was scandalized and the pair fled to Europe. Thus began Wright's long wilderness years.

Not that the trip to Europe was unproductive. The couple travelled widely, visiting Vienna where Wright saw the work of the Secessionists; Berlin, where he published two editions of his works with the publisher Ernst Wasmuth; Italy and France. Returning to America in 1911, Wright had neither clients nor money and so set about building himself and Mrs Cheney a home in southern Wisconsin on land owned by his mother's family. He called the house "Taliesin." Meaning "shining brow" in Welsh – a reference to the house's location on the crest of a hill – Taliesin was a retreat from the condemnatory world, a place of introspection and reflection, out of which the second great phase of Wright's career emerged.

Taliesin (or Taliesin East as it later became known) was a mythical place for Wright. The landscape around it was that of his forefathers and of his childhood (Wright spent his school holidays working on his uncles' farms); the rolling Wisconsin countryside brought out a shift in his architecture, the forceful horizontal lines of the Prairie houses gradually giving way to something that was altogether softer and more organic – more ancient, even. This period of Wright's work also sees a renewed interest in ornament. Spurred on perhaps by the work of the Viennese Secessionists, Wright's few commissions were intensely decorated, often with motifs drawn from Ancient American art. It is as if Taliesin reconnected Wright not only to his own history but to all history, albeit in a thoroughly modern way. The first public appearance of this new style was the Midway Gardens (1913–1914) in Chicago. The pleasure gardens were designed along the lines of the Austrian beer gardens Wright had seen on the Continent, and became a fashionable meeting place, complete with dance floors and an orchestra pit as well as vast in- and outdoor terraces for year-round use. Built of concrete and ceramic tiles, the gardens were a riot of decoration, Wright ornamenting every surface, giving the place the appearance of a rich tapestry, alive with patterns and textures.

The project that sustained Wright through these lean years, however, was the Imperial Hotel in Tokyo (1912–1923). Wright had visited Japan in 1905. When he won the commission to design the Imperial Hotel in 1912 it was a godsend: not only was the project prestigious and complex – the site was next to the Imperial Palace and in a notorious earthquake zone – it also provided Wright with on-going work. The hotel is a stunning combination of technical innovation and traditional Japanese design. Fabulously decorated inside and out – right down to the furniture – it was one of the few buildings to survive the disastrous 1923 earthquake thanks to its ingenious flexible foundations, and subsequently earned itself a reputation as a lucky place to get married.

Wright himself was not so lucky in love. In 1914 he hit the headlines again when a servant deliberately set fire to Taliesin East, killing seven people including Mrs Cheney. Unkind critics commented that it was Wright's retribution for abandoning his family for an adulterous rela-tionship. Undeterred, Wright immediately set about rebuilding Taliesin East, as he did the after it burned down a second time in 1924. For all his determination and drive, though, and for all his arrogance and seeming self-confidence, Wright was a man in need of female admiration and approval. Shortly after Mrs Cheney's death, he embarked on a disastrous rela-tionship with Miriam Noel, a stranger who had written him a letter of condolence. The pair were married but it was not a success: Noel was addicted to morphine and mentally unstable. When Wright began a relationship with Olgivanna Hinzenberg, a Montenegran dancer and disciple of Russian mystic Gurdieff, Noel stalked the couple, had Wright thrown into jail and hounded Olgivanna out of hospital when she gave birth to Wright's seventh child. He divorced Noel in 1927 and married Olgivanna the following year.

Work was thin on the ground throughout the 1920s, the Depression coupled with his scandal-ridden private life ensured that few clients came knocking at his door. Anyone else might have retired, but Wright holed up at the ever-expanding Taliesin East and continued to work furiously, churning out endless schemes for buildings that were never built and experi-menting with new technologies.

Besides the continuing work in Japan, Wright built a number of houses in California during this period. Known as the "textile block" houses, these large private residences were made from a system of reinforced concrete "textile" blocks that Wright created; they were not altogether unreminiscent of the simple Froebel blocks of his childhood. Describing the process of designing "La Miniatura", the house he designed for Alice Millard, Wright explained: "Gradually I unfolded to her the scheme of the textile block-slab house gradually forming in my mind since I got home from Japan. She wasn't frightened by the idea. Not at all."

Perhaps Mrs Millard should have been frightened. For what Wright had come up with was a radically new form of construction that, like so many of his inventions, did not wear altogether well. Intended to be easily assembled by a single unskilled labourer, the 16-inch (40-cm) square concrete blocks were placed one on top of the other and woven together like a piece of fabric by a system of slender interconnecting steel rods – the warp and woof of the structure.

"Concrete IS A PLASTIC MATERIAL – SUSCEPTIBLE TO THE IMPRESS OF THE IMAGINATION WHICH [IF MOULDED IN PIECES] IS PERMANENT, NOBLE, BEAUTIFUL ... cheap."

Wright's system had plenty of technical problems; the houses – like so many of his buildings – have needed constant attention. But certainly there is something noble, monumental even, about the textile block houses. The blocks themselves were either plain or embossed with motifs inspired by nature and the art of the pre-Columbus era, resulting in majestically robust-looking houses whose façades are nevertheless animated by stunning abstract decorated compositions.

Wright was one of the most innovative house designers of the twentieth century, constantly refining his idea of what a home should look like, but his vision was bigger than the individual dwelling. In 1932 he began work on Broadacre City, a blueprint for an ideal way of living. Today, Broadacre City seems horribly prophetic: a foretaste of the suburban sprawl that obliterates so much of America and the rest of the developed world. But in its time, Wright's masterplan was radical. Taking the car – the new "democratic" form of transport – as his starting point, Wright envisaged most of north America – excluding, for some reason, New England – divided up into a continuous grid of low-rise regional settlements comprising individual one acre lots.

The city of the future will be "so greatly different from the ancient city or from any city of today that we will probably fail to recognize its coming as the city at all," Wright wrote in

The Disappearing City, his first book on city planning. "America needs no help to build Broadacre City. It will build itself, haphazardly". Wright may not have set out to realize Broadacre City but the ideas behind it were incorporated into yet another housing prototype – a series of small suburban houses he designed during the 1930s called the "Usonian" houses.

Usonian – the word is a synthesis of USA and Utopia – was an adjective coined by Samuel Butler, a neologism to describe an ideal America. Wright took it up to describe a new type of house in his repertoire: a middle-class home without servants quarters, with a single living room in place of the traditional parlour and reception room, and carport instead of stable and garage. "Form and functions are one," Wright declared, twisting Sullivan's famous saying, "form follows function".

Wright built 20 Usonian houses in total but the house for which he continues to be best remembered is another one from this period: Fallingwater. Wright was into his late sixties when Edgar J. Kaufmann approached him in 1934. Work had picked up a little but, for an architect of his stature, designing inexpensive middle-class homes was not ideal. However, when Kaufmann showed him the site at Bear Run, Pennsylvania, Wright realized this was the project he had been waiting for.

"**FALLINGWATER** IS A GREAT BLESSING – ONE OF THE GREATEST BLESSINGS TO BE EXPERIENCED HERE ON EARTH, I THINK NOTHING YET EVER EQUALLED THE CO-ORDINATION [AND] SYMPATHETIC expression OF THE GREAT PRINCIPLE OF REPOSE WHERE FOREST AND STREAM AND ROCK AND ALL THE elements OF STRUCTURE ARE COMBINED SO QUIETLY THAT REALLY YOU LISTEN NOT TO ANY NOISE WHATSOEVER ALTHOUGH THE MUSIC OF THE STREAM IS THERE. BUT YOU LISTEN TO FALLINGWATER THE WAY YOU LISTEN TO THE QUIET OF THE COUNTRY." — WRIGHT TO HIS STUDENTS

And you have to agree with him.

Dubbed "the most famous house in the world today" by *House and Home* magazine in 1958, Fallingwater (1934–1937) was conceived in a single day. As legend has it Kaufmann, anxious that he had seen no drawings or preparatory sketches since their initial visit to the site, met Wright and asked what he was planning. Sitting down, Wright produced the design for Fallingwater straight off.

And yet, it had taken a lifetime to get to Fallingwater. The building is the culmination of Wright's concern to marry architecture and nature and, in so doing, to bring man closer to a spiritual understanding of the world. Cantilevered over a waterfall, the house seems to grow directly out of the rockbed, fanning out in a series of cascading terraces where one can sit and admire the dramatic view. Dispensing with ornament, Wright let the materials speak for themselves. Bringing the outside world in, as well as extending the house to the outdoors, he finished the interiors with rough stone walls and flagging so that the whole place feels like the inside of a cave.

To help him through the lean times of the 1920s Wright had set up the Taliesin Fellowship – a canny ploy to get students and young architects to pay to come and work for him. In the mid-1930s, his health deteriorating, Wright decided to decamp. The whole entourage – Wright, Olgivanna and students – headed west, to the warm desert climate of Arizona where, with the help of the Taliesin fellows, Wright designed and built his third home: the winter residence, Taliesin West.

It is as though the Taliesin East period had been a time of gestation. Thirty years after he first caught the world's attention with his Prairie houses, Wright again achieved worldwide recognition. Fallingwater was hailed as a masterpiece and in 1938 he appeared on the cover of *Time* magazine. In 1941, the Museum of Modern Art in New York dedicated an exhibition to his work. Wright was now well into his late sixties, yet he still had two of his best-known buildings ahead of him: the Johnson Wax building and the Guggenheim Museum.

A friend of Wright's, Herbert Johnson was a wealthy industrialist who had helped fund the Taliesin Fellowship. In 1936 he asked Wright to design a new administration building and laboratories for his family business – the massively successful Johnson Wax Company. Like Fallingwater, the Johnson Wax headquarters (1936–50) is one of the iconic buildings of the twentieth century. The complex – which, like so many Wright buildings, ran staggeringly over budget – was built in two phases: first the low, ground-hugging administration centre, then the 14-storey tower of laboratories. As different from each other as it is possible to get, the two buildings form an extraordinary composition, each playing with ideas of transparency: the lily-pad columns in the administration building holding up a glass roof that brings light flooding into the windowless interior; the 14-storey tower sheathed in horizontal bands of Pyrex glass tubing.

When anyone asked Wright which was his greatest building, his reply was always the same: "my next one". So it is fitting that Wright's last building should also be his most famous. As with almost every other building he designed, the Guggenheim Museum (1943–1959) in New York turns conventional forms upside down. In place of rectangular galleries piled on top of on another, Wright created a stunningly abstract building. Like the Froebel blocks of his childhood, the museum has at its heart a strong geometric element: in this case, a spiralling ramp that forms the main gallery space. Artists have argued over the merits of the building as a space in which to show art since the opening night. What is sure, though, is that the Guggenheim is one of the most impressive spaces in architectural history, visited by millions of art-lovers every year.

Wright died in 1959, just in time to see his masterpiece completed and his place in the history books assured. He is undoubtedly one of the great twentieth-century architects – indeed one of the great architects of all time. Many of his buildings have structural failings but it is the vision that counts: the vision to break through the rigid boxy style of nineteenth-century architecture and see that buildings can be so much more complex and fluid, so much more alive with possibility, so much in harmony with their natural environment. At this, Wright excelled. And in his own personal style, in his arrogance and ambition, his irreverence for social conventions, Wright anticipated the high-handed behaviour we have come to expect of great architects. He may not be the greatest architect of all time, but he's up there.

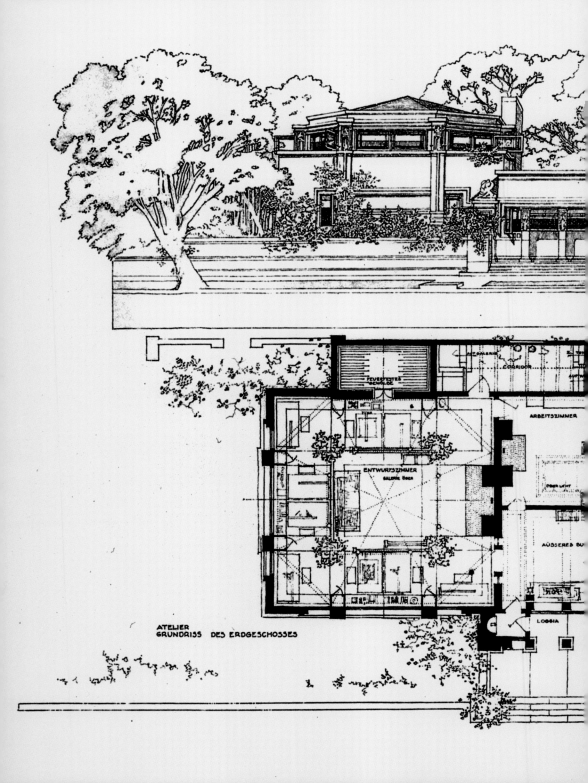

ATELIER
GRUNDRISS DES ERDGESCHOSSES

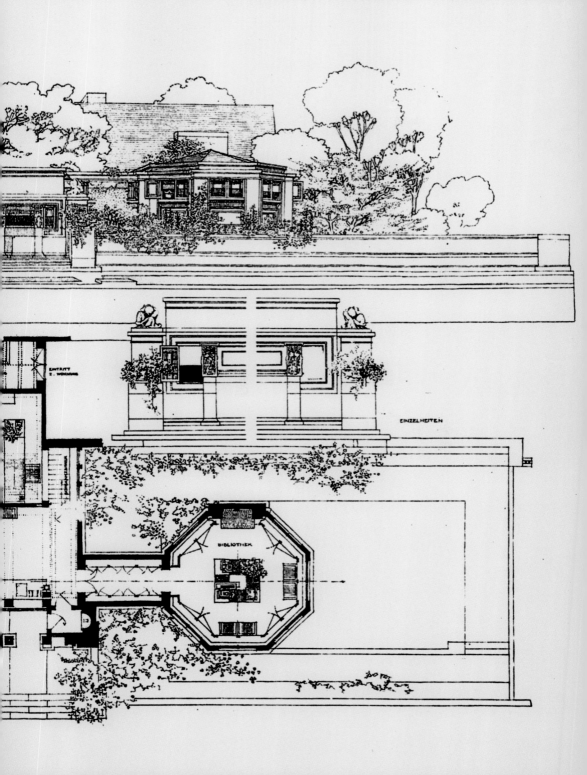

EINTRITT
Z. WOHNUNG

EINZELHEITEN

BIBLIOTHEK

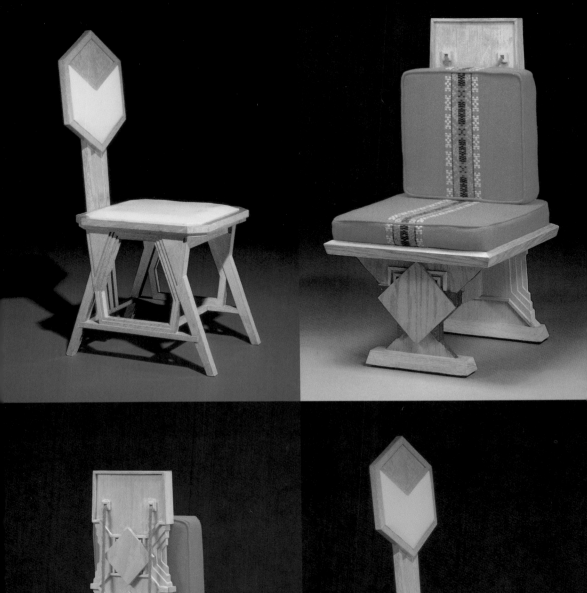

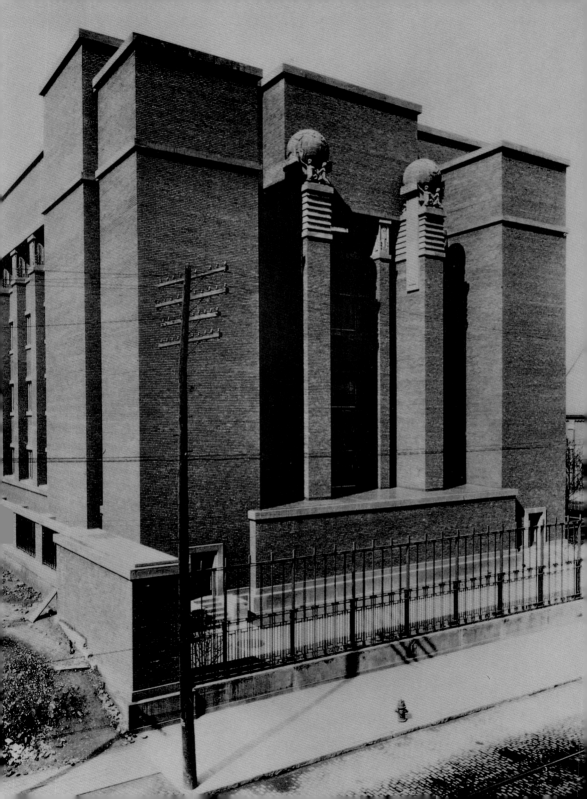

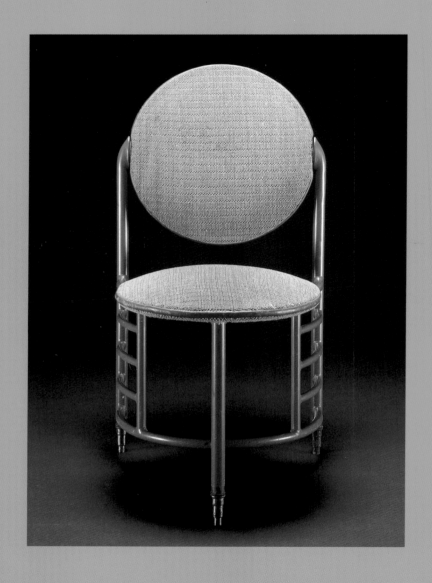

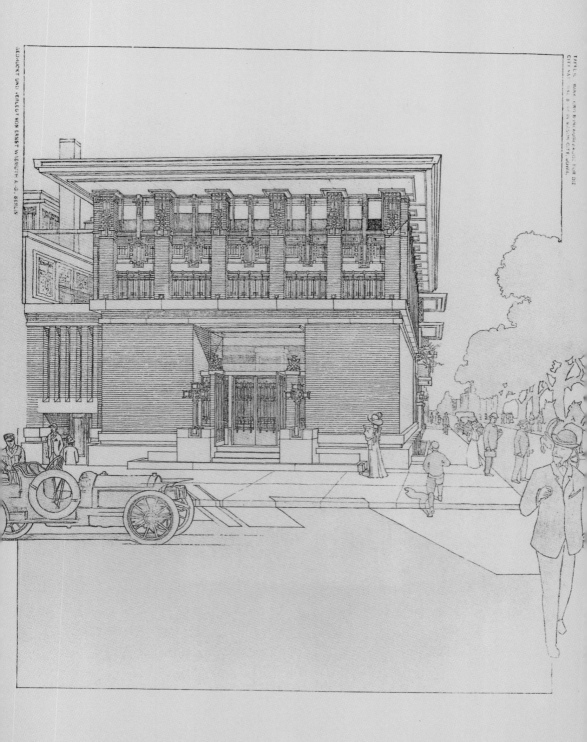

GEDRUCKT UND VERLEGT VON ERNST WASMUTH A. G. BERLIN

Private
Drive
Employees
Only

SC Johnson

No
Par

SOLOMON R GUGGENHEIM MUSEUM

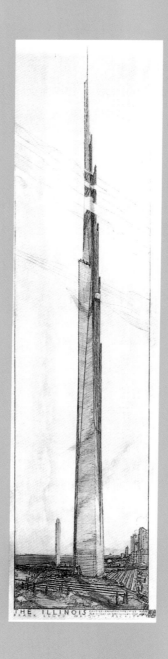

THE ILLINOIS
FRANK LLOYD WRIGHT ARCHITECT

STORER HOUSE

In California, Wright experimented with a new form of construction – textile block houses. These, like the 1923 Storer House, were yet another innovation in a long career of experimentation.

WRIGHT AT WORK

Frank Lloyd Wright in his drafting studio at Taliesin West, surrounded by the Taliesin Fellowship scholars.

BETH SHALOM SYNAGOGUE

Geometric forms remained at the heart of Wright's architecture, the Beth Shalom Synagogue (1954–59) is no exception.

GUGGENHEIM MUSEUM

The culmination of Wright's work, the spiralling Guggenheim Museum in New York (1943–59) was Wright's final building.

JOHNSON WAX BUILDING

The other great piece of Wright's late architecture, the Johnson Wax building (1936–39), is one of the twentieth century's great buildings.

WRIGHT RESIDENCE

The house that Frank Lloyd Wright built for himself and his family in Oak Park, Chicago (1889–1909) marks the start of his Prairie style.

WRIGHT RESIDENCE

The house at Oak Park evolved gradually, Wright adding a drafting studio after being fired by Louis Sullivan.

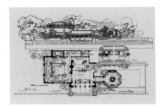

OAK PARK STYLE

Left: The rear view of the Wright residence. Right: Wright believed in the concept of the "total work of art" – designing the furniture (much of it terribly uncomfortable) for all his buildings.

AN EYE FOR DETAIL

While his buildings were shockingly unadorned for the time, Wright made considerable use of stained glass and simple patterns to lift his architecture.

WINSLOW AND HUSSER HOUSE

Wright's first solo building and the first true Prairie House, the Winslow House (1893–4), front and rear seen left, created a scandal when it was built.
Right: Furniture from the Husser House (1899).

UNITY TEMPLE

All concrete and fortress-like from the outside, Unity Temple (1905–08) is full of light inside. Again, Wright designed all the fittings, including the lights (right).

LARKIN BUILDING

A great cliff of a building from the outside, the Larkin Building in Buffalo, New York (1903–05) had a democratic open-plan office space, where everyone could see everyone else.

STEEL FURNITURE/CITY NATIONAL BANK

Wright's steel furniture for the Larkin Building, left, was revolutionary. Right, an image of the City National Bank in Mason City, Iowa, from the monographs published with Wasmuth in Berlin.

AVERY COONELY HOUSE

One of the most poetic of the Oak Park period houses – the Avery Coonely house (1907–08) at Riverside, Illinois.

THE ROBIE HOUSE

Dubbed the "battleship", the Robie House (1908–10) marks the apotheosis of Wright's Prairie style.

ROBIE HOUSE

Interior of the Robie House.

TALIESIN EAST

Returning from Europe with Mrs Cheney, Wright built a new home
– Taliesin East (1911–1925) – at Spring Green, Wisconsin on land
owned by his mother.

IMPERIAL HOTEL/HOLLYHOCK HOUSE

The Imperial Hotel Japan (1912–23), left above, for which Wright
even designed the china, left below, stimulated his interest in
ornament, as seen in the Hollyhock House (right, 1917).

STORER HOUSE

The Storer House (1923) is one of the best examples of Wright's
textile block construction: an astonishingly rich and complex
building.

STORER HOUSE

The building marks the renaissance of Wright's interest in
decoration – particularly in abstracted natural forms.

STORER HOUSE

The unpainted textile blocks were quick and easy to assemble by a single workman. Their rich patterning is reminiscent of Mayan details.

FALLINGWATER

One of the greatest houses of the century, Fallingwater (1934–37) is the point at which building and landscape merge into a seamless whole.

FALLINGWATER

Cascading terraces an interiors of rough stone walls characterize Wright's masterpiece.

USONIAN HOUSE

Simple and compact, the Pope Leighey House (1939) is typical of Wright's Usonian houses: good quality homes for the middle-classes.

TALIESIN WEST

Built by himself and his students in the Arizona desert, Taliesin West (1937–38) was Wright's third and most dramatic home.

JOHNSON WAX BUILDING

With its low administration building and glass research tower, the Johnson Wax building in Racine, Wisconsin (1936–50) is one of Wright's most dramatic compositions.

JOHNSON WAX BUILDING/PRICE TOWER

Geometry at work: Wright's love of abstracted natural forms and geometric patterns can be seen in the interior of the Johnson Wax building, left, and at the Price Tower, Oklahoma (1952–56).

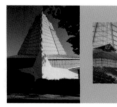

BETH SHALOM SYNAGOGUE

Made of a translucent cladding material, Wright's Beth Shalom Synagogue in Pennsylvania (1954–59) is filled with natural light.

GUGGENHEIM MUSEUM

An upturned ziggurat in form, the Guggenheim Museum in New York (1943–59) pushed Wright's interest in geometric forms to a new limit.

GUGGENHEIM MUSEUM

Inside, the building's spiralling ramp is the main gallery space, with pictures displayed on its continuous curving slope.

MILE HIGH TOWER/MARIN COUNTY CIVIC CENTRE

Wright's Mile High Tower, left, (1956) was never built although his space-ship of a building, the Marin County Civic Centre, California (1957) was.

Picture credits

The publishers would like to thank
the following sources for their
kind permission to reproduce the
pictures in this book:

AKG London 30b, Tony Vaccaro
   56t, 65
Arcaid/Richard Bryant 1, 5, 40-3,
   48-52, 58-9, 66-7, 69, 70-1,
   Scott Frances/Esto 54-5, Farrell
   Grehan 8-9, 44, 45, 62-3, Ezra
   Stoller/Esto 56b, 57, 60-1
Christie's Images Ltd. 27, 28, 31,
   36, 46b
Corbis UK/Bettmann 2-3, 38-9,
   46t, Sandy Felsenthal 22-3, 26,
   29, 33, Michael Freeman 47, 53,
   G.E. Kidder Smith 64, Gail
   Mooney 7, Ted Streshinsky 73,
   Roger Wood 68,
Royal Institute of British
   Architects 24-5, 30t, 34, 35, 37,
   72